Welcome to FACTopia, where each fact leads on to the next in endlessly entertaining ways!

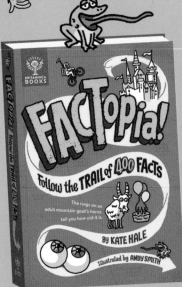

FACTopia!
Follow the TRAIL of 400 FACTS
The rings on an adult mountain goat's horns tell you how old it is.
BY KATE HALE
Illustrated by ANDY SMITH

RETURN TO FACTopia!
Follow the TRAIL of 400 MORE FACTS
At night, giraffes quietly hum to one another.
BY KATE HALE
Illustrated by ANDY SMITH

GROSS FACTopia!
Follow the TRAIL of 400 FOUL FACTS
Hippopotamuses spin their tails while they poop.
BY PAIGE TOWLER
Illustrated by ANDY SMITH

ANIMAL FACTopia!
Follow the TRAIL of 400 BEASTLY FACTS
Chameleons change the color of their skin to help them cool down.
BY JULIE BEER
Illustrated by ANDY SMITH

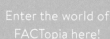

BRITANNICA BOOKS

HISTORY FACTOPia!

Follow ye Olde TRAIL of 400 FACTS

By PAIGE TOWLER

Illustrated by ANDY SMITH

CONTENTS

Travel back in time to FACTopia!

Get ready: Things are about to get old-school on a fun-filled journey through human history.

This blast-from-the-past adventure takes you through hundreds of the most mind-blowing, wow-worthy, and crazy-cool facts from yesteryear. For example...

Archaeologists in China found a 3,300-year-old pair of pants—the oldest ever discovered.

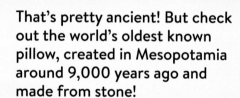

That's pretty ancient! But check out the world's oldest known pillow, created in Mesopotamia around 9,000 years ago and made from stone!

Speaking of stone... In 1799, French emperor Napoleon's soldiers discovered the Rosetta Stone—a carved slab that allowed scholars to translate ancient Egyptian hieroglyphics.

While we're in Egypt, according to one historian, ancient Egyptians may have sung to pet lions while feeding them.

Purrrr. In 1949, a ship's cat named Simon was awarded a medal for raising morale and keeping ships rat free...

You might have spotted that there is something special about being here in FACTopia. Every fact is linked to the next, and in the most surprising and even hilarious ways.

On this historical FACTopia tour, you will encounter radical rulers, fantastic fashion, wondrous warriors, historic heists, and... well, you'll see. Discover what each turn of the page will bring!

But there isn't just one trail through this book. Your path branches every now and then, and you can zip forward and zoom backward to go to a totally different (but still connected) part of FACTopia. →

Let your curiosity take you wherever it leads. Of course, a good place to start could be right here, at the beginning........

For example, set sail on this detour to

find out about pirates.

Go to page 22

Nearly 3,000 years ago, during the **early Olympics**, athletes competed naked...

Spectacular sports

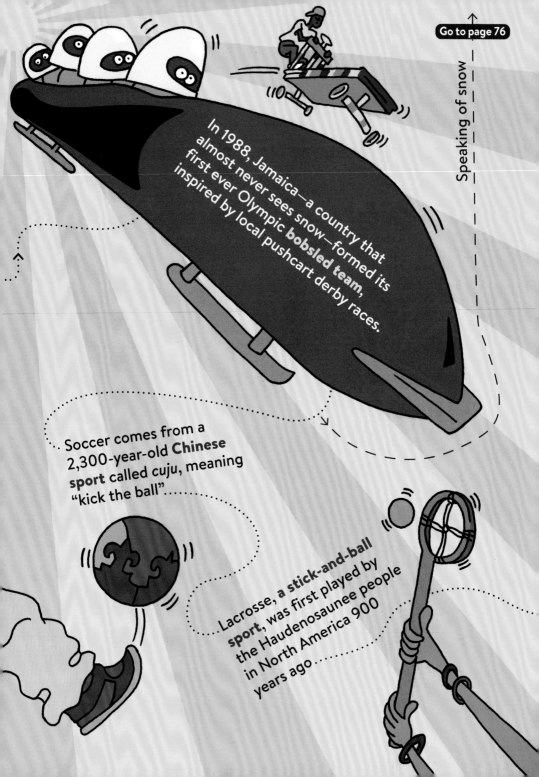

Go to page 76

Speaking of snow

In 1988, Jamaica—a country that almost never sees snow—formed its first ever Olympic **bobsled team**, inspired by local pushcart derby races.

Soccer comes from a 2,300-year-old **Chinese sport** called cuju, meaning "kick the ball".

Lacrosse, **a stick-and-ball sport**, was first played by the Haudenosaunee people in North America 900 years ago

In the 1700s, Argentina's national sport, *pato*, involved players passing around a duck in a basket. Now, they shoot a ball into hoops from **horseback**...

Giddyup

In the 1890s, a deaf football player named Paul Hubbard invented the **huddle** to keep his hand signals secret from the other teams...

In 1969, one businessman flew racehorses around the world in a plane called **Air Horse One**—based on the U.S. presidential plane Air Force One—complete with in-flight meals.

Go to page 42

Soar through the skies

Dress to impress

Starting around the
15th century, some
horse-face armor used
throughout Europe
and Asia made horses
look like dragons,
unicorns, and more.

....Nineteenth-century warriors from Kiribati,
an island nation in the Pacific Ocean, wore

SPIKY HELMETS

made from blowfish...

See the seas

Go to page 142

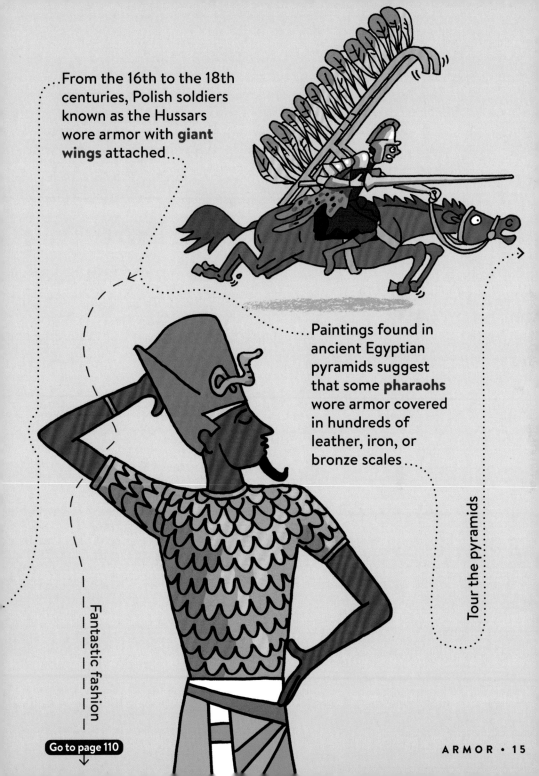

From the 16th to the 18th centuries, Polish soldiers known as the Hussars wore armor with **giant wings** attached...

Paintings found in ancient Egyptian pyramids suggest that some **pharaohs** wore armor covered in hundreds of leather, iron, or bronze scales...

Tour the pyramids

Fantastic fashion

Go to page 110

Go to page 52

That's huge!

...In Mexico, archaeologists uncovered the **largest pyramid** in the world hidden inside a hill. Built some 2,300 years ago, the Great Pyramid of Cholula has a base as long as nine Olympic-size swimming pools...

...Scientists discovered a hidden chamber in the Great Pyramid of Giza using **cosmic rays** from space! The rays can penetrate stone to create an image just like X-rays in our body...

Discover more

Go to page 128

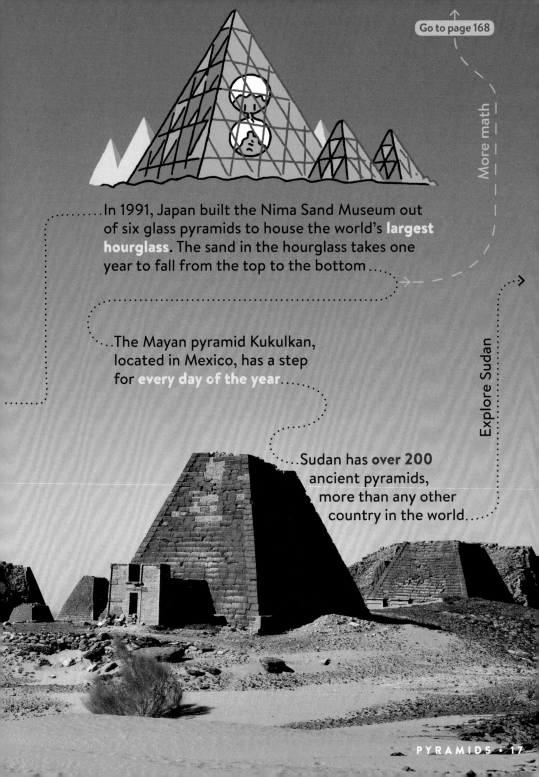

Go to page 168

More math

In 1991, Japan built the Nima Sand Museum out of six glass pyramids to house the world's **largest hourglass**. The sand in the hourglass takes one year to fall from the top to the bottom

The Mayan pyramid Kukulkan, located in Mexico, has a step for **every day of the year**

Explore Sudan

Sudan has **over 200** ancient pyramids, more than any other country in the world

In Sudan, one 2,300-year-old pharaoh's tomb can be accessed only by using an air tube to dive deep underwater.

A ruler of the Moche people, an ancient civilization from Peru, was buried in a lavish tomb alongside gold, jewels, and what may have been his favorite pet dog.

When the toilet system on the space shuttle *Discovery* malfunctioned in 1984, a large icicle made of pee formed on its exterior due to the freezing temperatures in space.

From space, you can see the enormous moat around Cambodia's 800-year-old Angkor Wat temple.

The moats around medieval European castles often contained the waste from the castle's toilets.

The Swedish Vallhund, a type of **dog** said to be originally bred by the **Vikings**, looks like a mix between a Corgi and a wolf.

Because urine was used and sold for many purposes, the ancient Roman **government** imposed a tax on **pee** collected from public toilets.

After **Vikings** settled in Iceland, they founded a type of **government** around the year 930 that is still in use in the country today—making it one of the oldest existing governments in the world.

The show must go on

Workers renovating a 14th-century **castle** in Romania discovered a secret escape passage **hidden** behind a fireplace.

Built in 1896, a theater **hidden** beneath a Boston piano shop held concerts and opera performances four stories underground.

In 1939, Chickasaw actress Te Ata performed her **one-woman show** celebrating Chickasaw stories and other Native American traditions for President Franklin D. Roosevelt and his guests, King George VI and Queen Elizabeth the Queen Mother.

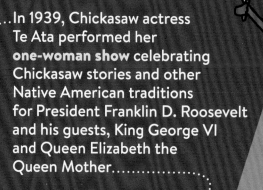

William Shakespeare's play *Macbeth* is said to have been cursed since its first performance in 1606. Many actors now avoid saying its name and instead call it **"the Scottish Play".**

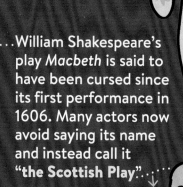

More curses

Go to page 132

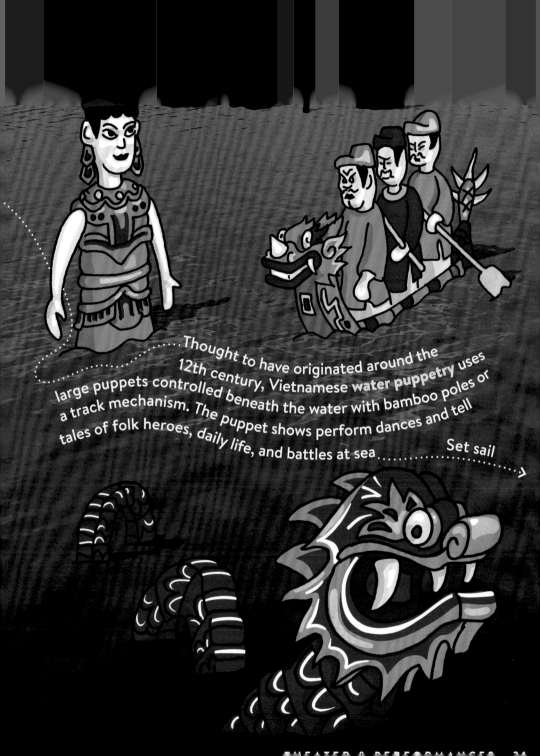

Thought to have originated around the 12th century, Vietnamese water puppetry uses large puppets controlled beneath the water with bamboo poles or a track mechanism. The puppet shows perform dances and tell tales of folk heroes, daily life, and battles at sea..............Set sail

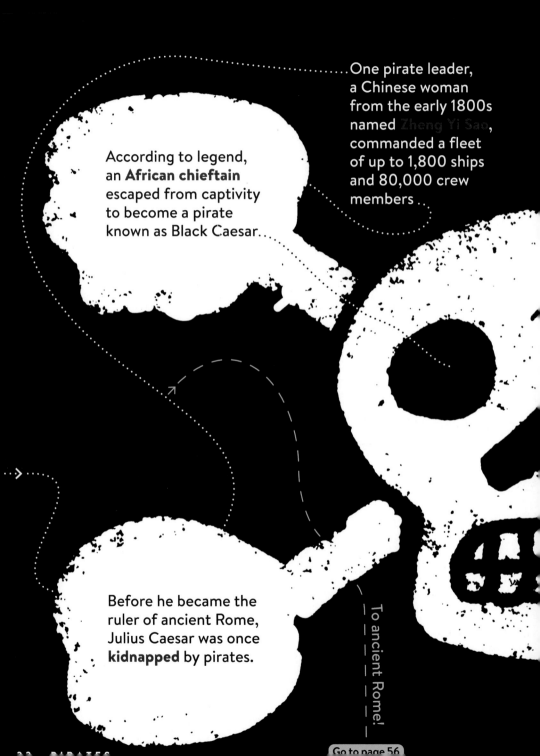

One pirate leader, a Chinese woman from the early 1800s named Zheng Yi Sao, commanded a fleet of up to 1,800 ships and 80,000 crew members.

According to legend, an **African chieftain** escaped from captivity to become a pirate known as Black Caesar.

Before he became the ruler of ancient Rome, Julius Caesar was once **kidnapped** by pirates.

To ancient Rome!

Go to page 56

In the late 1800s in Chesapeake Bay, in Maryland and Virginia, pirates battled for control of the area's oyster trade—an event known as the **Oyster Wars**.

In 1681, English pirates captured 700 **slabs of silver** from a Spanish ship, but abandoned the treasure because they thought it was useless tin!

To battle

Go to page 146

Arrive in Australia

King Louis Philippe of France once declared war on Mexico over a disagreement about a pastry restaurant.

Time for dessert ⟩

In 1932, the Australian government declared war on the country's emus.

Pavlova, a dessert made from meringue, cream, and fruit, was supposedly created in New Zealand in the 1920s to look like Russian ballerina **Anna Pavlova's** tutu

Dance this way

Go to page 190

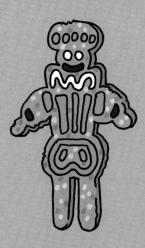

Queen Elizabeth I impressed visiting foreign noblemen with **gingerbread men** made to look like them.

Nearly 2,500 years ago, the Maya used **hot chocolate** to help cure rashes and fevers.

According to legend, a Turkish dessert called *tavuk göğsü*—which combines **sweet pudding with chicken**—was created when an Ottoman sultan asked for a sweet late-night snack.

Inspired by a trip to Europe in the mid-1900s, a Japanese baker created the soufflé cheesecake—a cheesecake that **wiggles**.

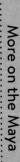More on the Maya

The ancient Mayan **hieroglyphic** writing system included more than 800 signs.

Go to page 114

Read on

The Maya were making **rubber balls** for sports nearly 3,000 years before rubber was "invented" in the U.S.A.

The ancient Maya created a **rain festival** called Pa Puul, still observed today, which involves breaking clay pots to copy the sound of thunder.

Let's party!

Since 1922, a town in El Salvador has celebrated Bolas de Fuego, a festival during which participants **throw fireballs** made of flaming cloth to remember a 1658 volcanic eruption

In 1897, the mayor of Oaxaca, Mexico, created **Night of the Radishes**—an annual radish-carving celebration

People in Nepal celebrate Kukur Tihar to honor dogs—considered the messengers of the god of death—by dressing them in **flower necklaces** and preparing special meals for them

Woof

The ancestors of **Rhodesian ridgebacks** were dogs that were bred in what is now the country of Zimbabwe to protect their owners from lions.

In 1928, Buddy, one of the first **Seeing Eye dogs** in the U.S.A., led his owner Morris Frank down a busy New York City street.

In ancient Aztec and Maya cultures, people believed that the Xoloitzcuintli, a type of **hairless dog**, guarded the living and guided the dead to the underworld.

In 1960, two **Soviet dogs**, Belka and Strelka, were the first dogs to survive being sent into space. They orbited Earth 17 times, then safely returned home....

Blast off!

The world's oldest known dog breed, **the Saluki**, was so revered in ancient Egypt that pharaohs kept these dogs as pets.

In 1961, the **first person** ever to go to space, Russian cosmonaut Yuri Gagarin, peed on his transport bus's right rear wheel before takeoff and started a new tradition.

A mysterious

explo

that flattened about 772 square miles (2,000sq km) of Siberian forest in 1908 could have been caused by a comet or asteroid exploding high up in Earth's atmosphere.

Go to page 120

sion

The first known reference to **extraterrestrials** is in an ancient Greek story about people who lived on the moon and whose sweat was made of milk.

We come in peace

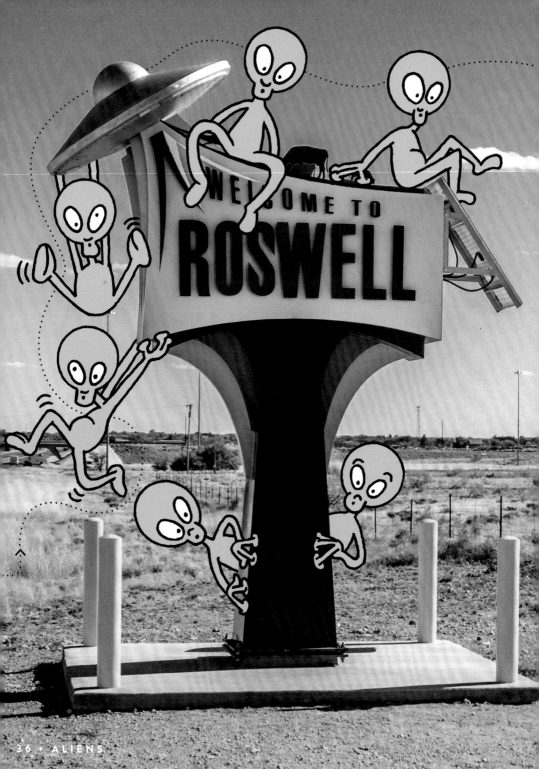

U F O

After an **U**nidentified **F**lying **O**bject crashed in Roswell, New Mexico, in 1947, people believed the town had been visited by aliens— but it was actually secret government technology

Is anybody out there?

In 1977, a space telescope known as Big Ear detected a mysterious signal that might have been from extraterrestrials. Scientists called it "Wow!"

The Itsekiri people of Nigeria have a tradition of building enormous canoes. Each **ship** is carved from a single tree, and some can hold more than 100 sailors.

In 1872, the *Mary Celeste*, a mysterious "ghost **ship**," was discovered floating at sea with nobody on board.

An 8,000-year-old recipe is the oldest ever found. It's for a savory pudding made from stinging nettle **leaves**.

In 1789, a London expert on sweets published a **Parmesan** cheese ice-cream recipe.

For thousands of years, Polynesian peoples have used large, strong Ti (or Ki) **leaves** to make roofs, fishing nets, ropes, clothing, and even shoes.

For centuries, people across North America, Europe, and Australia have hidden shoes in the walls of their homes, perhaps to ward off evil **spirits**.

A trickster **spirit** called the Bannik has visited bathhouses in northeastern Europe, at least according to legend.

Some sections of the Great **Wall** of China were built using rice flour paste.

Since the Iron and Bronze Ages, people have used tree trunks to build spike-topped **walls** called palisades.

A type of black rice is sometimes called "forbidden rice" as it was once reserved for only the **emperors** of ancient China.

Italian monks first made hard, salty **Parmesan** as a way to keep milk from going bad.

Chinese **Emperor** Jianwen's enemies burned down his palace. According to legend, he escaped the blaze disguised as a monk.

One legend says that the 2,000-year-old group of enormous stone **jars** found in Laos were left behind by partying giants who had used them as cups.

A 2,000-year-old clay **jar** found in Iraq may have been used as a battery. The jar has an iron bar surrounded by copper at its center and can hold an electric charge when filled with an acid such as vinegar.

More amazing inventions

...>·····In the 1930s, a British inventor created the Dynasphere—
an **enormous wheel** with a driver inside

Snow goggles were invented more than 2,000 years ago in modern-day Alaska and Canada by the Inuit people and the Yupik people. They carved small slits into bone, leather, or wood to make eye masks

Nearly 2,000 years ago, an Egyptian woman known as Mary the Prophetess, invented the bain-marie, a method used in cooking and science for gently heating substances over boiling water.

In 1655, a German inventor created the first known **self-propelled wheelchair**— a carriage that moved when the driver turned a crank.

More than 1,000 years before the first airplane, Spanish inventor Abbas Ibn Firnas successfully created and piloted **a glider**.

Take to the air >

...A 16th-century scientist wore **fake wings** covered in feathers to try to fly from the top of a castle wall in Scotland. He blamed his failure on the fact that he had used feathers from a chicken, not an eagle........

During World War II, an all-female squad of Russian pilots were nicknamed the "Night Witches" because their planes made a whooshing noise similar to the sound of a sweeping broom.

Kites were invented in China some 2,200 years ago to send messages during wartime.

More on ancient China

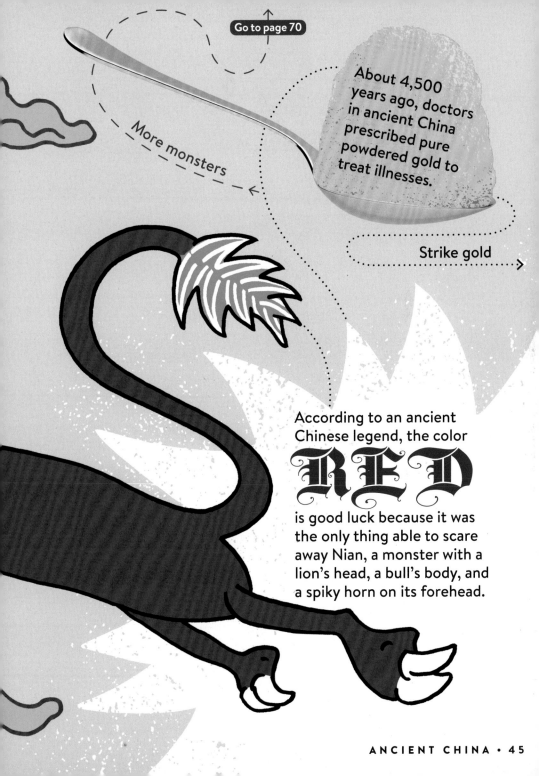

Go to page 70 ↑

About 4,500 years ago, doctors in ancient China prescribed pure powdered gold to treat illnesses.

More monsters ←

Strike gold →

According to an ancient Chinese legend, the color

RED

is good luck because it was the only thing able to scare away Nian, a monster with a lion's head, a bull's body, and a spiky horn on its forehead.

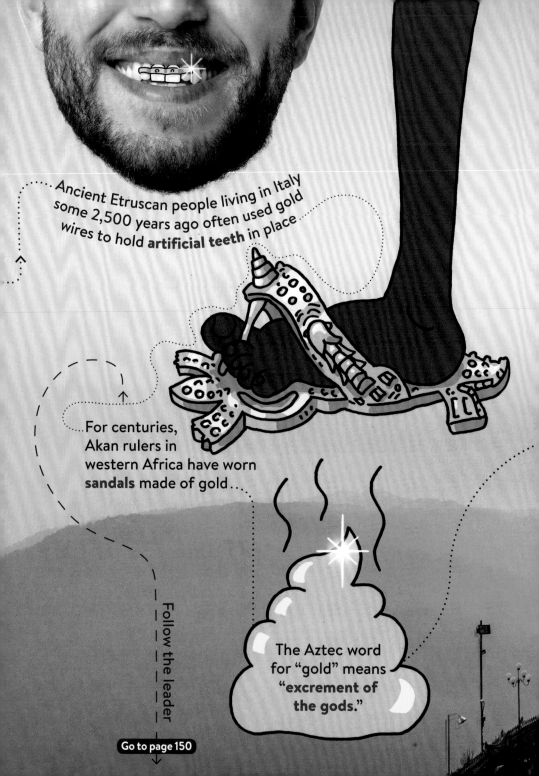

Ancient Etruscan people living in Italy some 2,500 years ago often used gold wires to hold **artificial teeth** in place...

For centuries, Akan rulers in western Africa have worn **sandals** made of gold...

The Aztec word for "gold" means "**excrement of the gods.**"

Follow the leader

Go to page 150

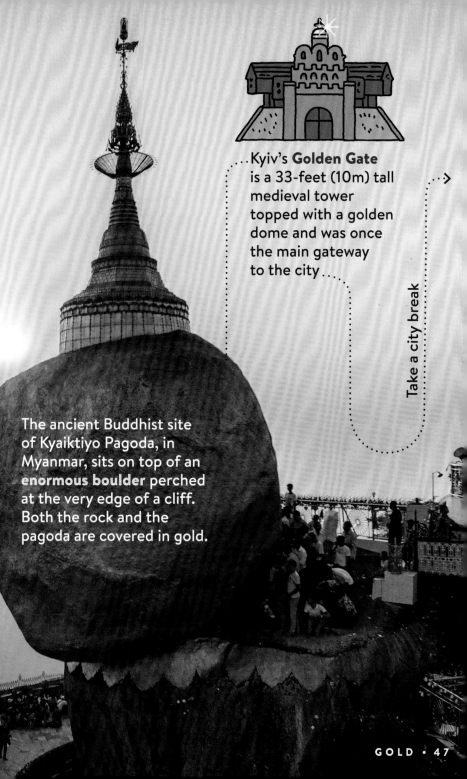

Kyiv's **Golden Gate** is a 33-feet (10m) tall medieval tower topped with a golden dome and was once the main gateway to the city

Take a city break

The ancient Buddhist site of Kyaiktiyo Pagoda, in Myanmar, sits on top of an **enormous boulder** perched at the very edge of a cliff. Both the rock and the pagoda are covered in gold.

A city in Yemen called Shibam consists almost entirely of **skyscrapers** built from mud in the 16th century.

More mud ·····→

Go to page 162

Get well soon

Scientists are considering bringing back the ancient treatment of covering wounds in **mud**, which can contain bacteria to fight infections.....

For centuries in Japan, people at the Paantu festival have dressed up as **masked spirits** and covered everything they can—including streets, cars, buildings, and people—in mud for good luck.

Found buried in mud in Cairo, Egypt, a **3,000-year-old** **statue** of a pharaoh was nearly two stories tall.

That's huge!

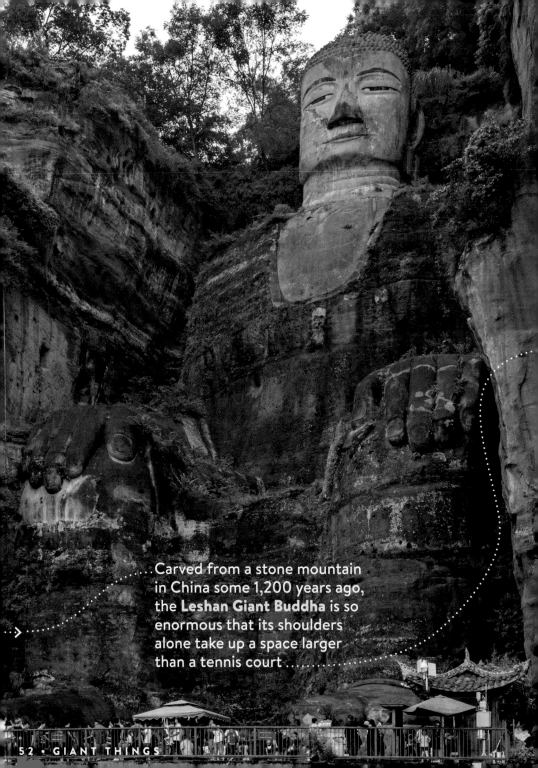

Carved from a stone mountain in China some 1,200 years ago, the **Leshan Giant Buddha** is so enormous that its shoulders alone take up a space larger than a tennis court

Go to page 10

Swing for sports

Archaeologists in Peru recently discovered 2,000-year-old art—featuring a **lounging cat**—the length of a Boeing 737 airplane and drawn into the side of a mountain.

How artistic

The first human **cannonball** was a **stuntwoman** named Rosa Richter, who was fired from a circus cannon in 1877.

Bessie Coleman, a 1920s Black Cherokee airplane **stuntwoman**, was the world's first licensed Black **pilot** and first licensed Indigenous American pilot.

Apparently, a portrait of **King** George II hanging in a hall in New Jersey was destroyed when a **cannonball** was shot through a window during the American Revolution.

Ninth-century Islamic ruler Hārūn al-Rashīd sent an **elephant** as a gift for Charlemagne, **king** of the Franks.

Ancient Roman and Greek **armies** may have used pigs to drive away enemy war **elephants**—which were scared of pigs' squeals.

In 1953, U.S. artist Robert Rauschenberg erased the priceless art of a famous Dutchman called Willem de Kooning, then hung the now-blank paper in a **museum**.

In 1980, Scotland opened an entire **museum** dedicated to the Loch Ness monster—a **mythical creature** said to live in Loch Ness, a large lake.

Feng Ru, a 1900s **pilot** who built the first airplanes in **China**, was said to be so secretive about his designs that he would speak to factory visitors only through a crack in the wall.

An early compass was created in **China** more than 2,000 years ago and featured a tiny **chariot** carrying a figure that always pointed south.

Worth about $15 billion in today's money, the highest-earning athlete in history may have been a **chariot** driver from ancient Rome.

All roads lead to....

Until a town witnessed more than 3,000 rocks falling from the sky in 1803, many **scientists** did not believe that **meteorites** came from outer space.

According to the ancient historian Plutarch, a **meteorite** fell during a battle in the first century BCE, causing the two **armies** to call off the conflict.

More than 51 million **trees** were planted in Kenya after **scientist** Wangarí Muta Maathai started an anti-deforestation movement in 1977.

The asema is a **mythical creature** from Suriname, and is said to be a shape-shifting **vampire** that can remove its skin.

In centuries-old Japanese folklore, the Jubokko is a **vampire tree** that drinks human blood.

Some ancient Romans dyed their hair using a mixture of vinegar and

ROTTEN LEECHES

Time for a trim? →

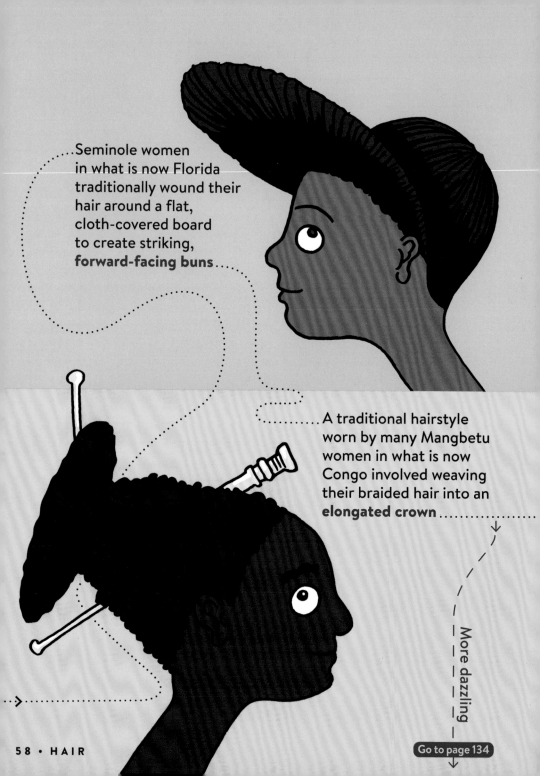

Seminole women in what is now Florida traditionally wound their hair around a flat, cloth-covered board to create striking, **forward-facing buns**...

A traditional hairstyle worn by many Mangbetu women in what is now Congo involved weaving their braided hair into an **elongated crown**..................

More dazzling

Go to page 134

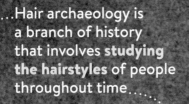

Hair archaeology is a branch of history that involves **studying the hairstyles** of people throughout time

Japanese samurai once commonly wore a hairstyle called the *chonmage*, which helped their **elaborate helmets** stay put

More samurai

During the Victorian era, some people in Europe and North America wore **jewelry** that displayed or was even made of human hair

Samurai—members of the **Japanese warrior** class that emerged in the late 1100s—were not only expected to be brave, disciplined, and loyal, but also to master arts such as poetry or *flower arranging*

Onna-bugeisha were fierce **female martial artists** who fought alongside samurai in battle

Put up your defenses

Go to page 122

The *bagh nakh*, developed in India by the 1600s, was a steel weapon made to look like a **tiger's claws**.

Adventure to India

Boomerangs have been used as hunting weapons for about 20,000 years, but not all of them are designed to come back. Some Aboriginal peoples used **returning boomerangs** to hunt birds.

According to a Maori chief who ruled in New Zealand in the late 1700s, his most **prized weapon**—a club made entirely of jade—could reveal the future by changing color.

Ancient slings could launch stone

Traditional **daggers and clubs** of the Tlingit people of North America often featured intricate carvings of animals, such as bears, birds, and wolves.

Find your creativity

projectiles to fly faster than a cheetah can run....

World-famous artist **Frida Kahlo** first began painting when she was stuck in bed following a bus accident in Mexico in 1925.

take nearly a year to complete.

Medieval marvels ....>

wampum beads

For centuries, many Native American nations in the northeastern U.S.A. and in Canada have crafted

—made from white and purple mollusk shells— and woven them into ceremonial belts that record historical events, laws, and traditions...

Strange illustrations found in medieval European manuscripts include a snail attacking a knight, animals playing instruments, walking fish, and animals and people passing gas.

In medieval Europe, dogs were allowed to **roam banquet halls** and clean up food scraps from the floor.

From the Middle Ages to the late 19th century, warriors—and their horses—across parts of sub-Saharan Africa often wore **brightly colored** cloth-quilted armor.

Going to the dogs

Go to page 32

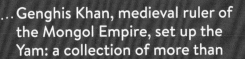

Genghis Khan, medieval ruler of the Mongol Empire, set up the Yam: a collection of more than

50,000 HORSES

that were used to create one of the first international mail systems

Rad rulers ⟩

In medieval Europe, women often **plucked their hairlines** to make their foreheads appear larger

England's Queen Elizabeth I bragged that she had wonderful hygiene because she bathed **once a month.**

Before she became queen, Cleopatra VII was exiled from Egypt, but was supposedly smuggled back into her palace **rolled up in a carpet**

The monstrous vampire

Dracula

may have been
inspired by real-life
Vlad Țepeș, a
15th-century
king of Walachia
(in present-
day Romania)······

That's monstrous!

.....⟩ In the late 19th and early 20th century in South Africa, there
were reported sightings of a **grootslang**—a mythical monster
with the head of an elephant and the body of a huge serpent—
believed to live inside a deep cave ....

Go underground

In 1920, a Russian **scientist** invented the theremin—a **musical instrument** that uses radio waves to make sound without being touched.

A cave full of Maya treasure was recently discovered under the ruins at Mexico's Chichén Itzá—**scientists** found a venomous snake guarding the entrance.

In the early 1900s, **street vendors** across the U.S.A. physically battled over territory and the right to sell the corn snacks **tamales**.

The ancient Aztecs invented a **tamale** **recipe** that includes axolotls, a type of salamander.

The perfume from a 500-year-old **recipe** created for the French queen Catherine de' Medici is still on sale at the **store** that originally made it in Florence, Italy.

The centuries-old kora, a **musical instrument** from western Africa with 21 strings, can sound like a harp or a guitar.

In 1815, the sound of a **volcanic eruption** from Indonesia's Mount Tambora could be heard over 1,200 miles (1,930km) away.

In 79CE, a **volcanic eruption** buried the Roman city of Pompeii. Archaeologists have since discovered traces of food left there on a street vendor's stand.

It's a sand storm

A **store** in Ireland features plexiglass floors, so shoppers can glimpse the 11th-century Viking ruins buried beneath.

Archaeologists believe ancient ruins in Oman could be Ubar, a city swallowed by desert sands and until now thought to exist only in legend.

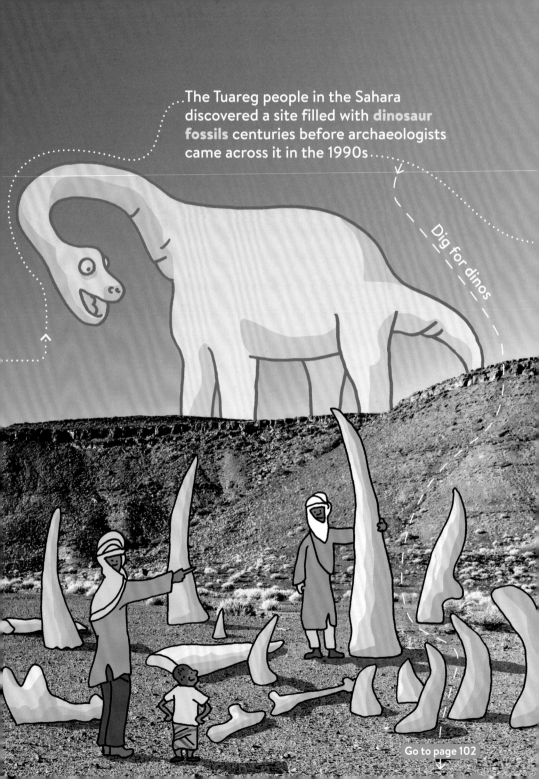

The Tuareg people in the Sahara discovered a site filled with **dinosaur fossils** centuries before archaeologists came across it in the 1990s.

Dig for dinos

Go to page 102

In a centuries-old tradition, Mongolian herders greet the New Year by riding **Bactrian camels** through the snows of the Gobi Desert...

Brrr! ....>

In 1953, Norway established a **school** that teaches the ancient Sami practice of reindeer herding.

In 1914, during World War I, British and German troops held a spontaneous truce at Christmas. They set up **Christmas trees** and played sports in the snow.

That's mechanical

The first **artificial snow** machine was invented in Hollywood in 1934 to create more realistic-looking winters for movies filmed in warm, sunny California.

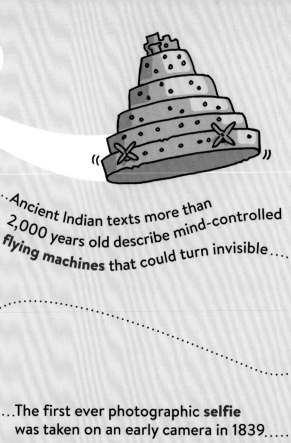

Ancient Indian texts more than 2,000 years old describe mind-controlled **flying machines** that could turn invisible

The first ever photographic **selfie** was taken on an early camera in 1839

Go to page 8

Fantastic firsts

For nearly 3,000 years, armies from Asia to Europe attacked castles using **siege towers**: towering machines that could hold hundreds of soldiers and be rolled up to castle walls.

Storm the ramparts!

Go to page 156

Here, kitty

Scotland's Edinburgh Castle was built on top of an **extinct volcano**.

Three separate castles built in Algeria in the

Founded in the 17th century by the ruler of Ethiopia, the fortress city Fasil Ghebbi was built to house the emperor, his family, his servants, and his **pet lions**

...16th century are all connected by **secret underground tunnels**...

In Japan, Matsumoto Castle has a **hidden level** where samurai could safely rest from their attackers because it has no windows

There's a 3,000-year-old castle at the **bottom of a lake** in Turkey...

Dive in! 〉

Over some 100 years, a ship that sank off the coast of Australia turned into an artificial coral reef, providing a home for lots of underwater life

Divers in Lithuania discovered the skeleton of a 16th-century soldier with his boots and sword still intact

Spooky skeletons

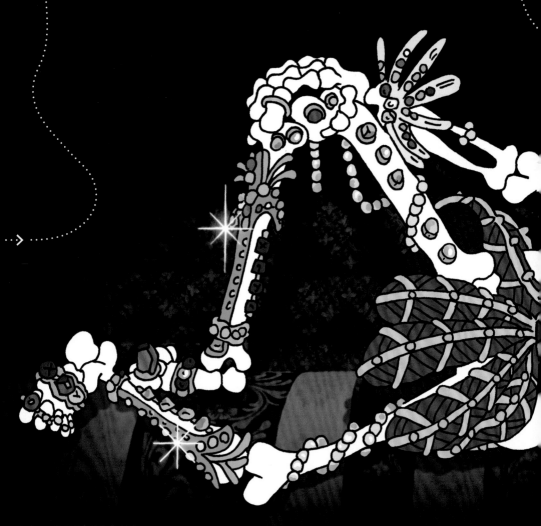

In 1578, workers discovered mysterious skeletons—believed to be the holy remains of lost saints—in the

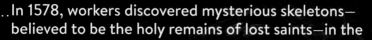

CATACOMBS

of Rome. The skeletons were sent to churches across Europe, where they were covered in gold clothing and jewels..........

So sparkly!

When the bubonic plague struck Europe in the 14th century, some people believed that eating a could be a cure

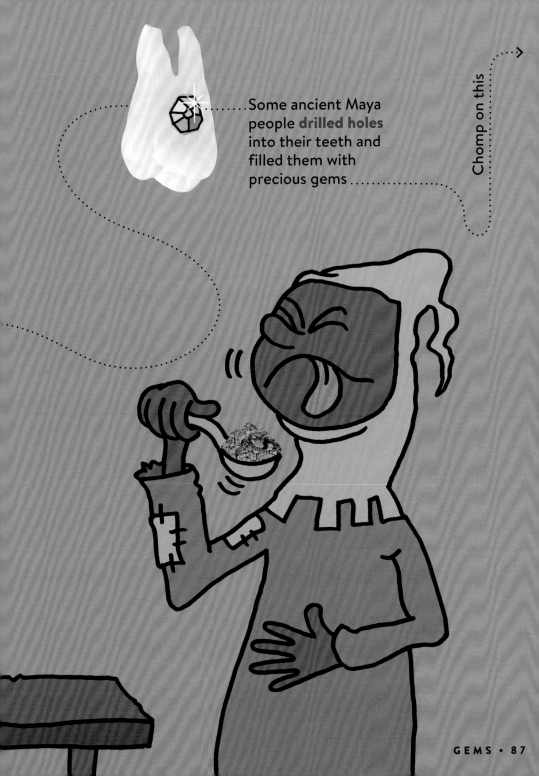

Some ancient Maya people **drilled holes** into their teeth and filled them with precious gems

Chomp on this

From ancient Madagascar to ancient Vietnam, and from Tudor England to medieval Japan, people across the world often **blackened their teeth** as a popular beauty trend

The Vikings sometimes used files to **carve deep lines** into their teeth—and may have even painted them

The Vikings may have **hunted** animals while skiing

Go to page 196

Play some games

Scientists believe that Viking tales of legendary **female fighters** called shield-maidens may have been inspired by real-life warrior women.

Fight on →

To start fires, Vikings often used a type of fungus that had been

BOILED IN PEE

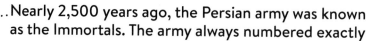

Nearly 2,500 years ago, the Persian army was known as the Immortals. The army always numbered exactly

10,000 SOLDIERS

—any who died were immediately replaced...

One of the most revered Mongols was Khutulun, a **warrior princess** who was also an undefeated wrestling champion...

...The Eagle Warriors were the most elite of all Aztec soldiers. They wore **feathered armor** and helmets shaped like eagle heads...

Awesome armor

Go to page 14

The Amazon warrior women in Greek mythology were likely based upon the female warriors of Scythia (in modern-day Central Asia and Eastern Europe)

Legendary!

The word "goth" comes from the Visigoths, a group of Germanic peoples whose warriors conquered Rome in 410

Go to page 184

Lost treasures

Known as the Oak Island Money Pit, a site in Nova Scotia, Canada, supposedly holds a **great treasure** buried more than 200 years ago—but it's said to be booby-trapped to flood whenever anyone digs too close.

A legend says Chinese writing was invented thousands of years ago by a man whose **four eyes** allowed him to see patterns other people couldn't

According to legend, 12th-century Empress Matilda was imprisoned in Oxford Castle,

...Historians thought that La Ciudad Blanca—a lost city in Central America made of **shining white stones**—was made up. But recently, archaeologists have discovered a lost city in Honduras that may have inspired the tale...

Feeling lost?

In one Polish legend, the founder of the city of Kraków **slew a dragon** by stuffing a sheep hide with the chemical sulfur, which exploded after the dragon ate it.

England, but escaped by **skating** across the frozen River Thames in the middle of the night...

Go to page 104

Archaeologists in South Africa discovered the lost 15th-century city of Kweneng using

LASERS

More maps

Rock Summit

What's in the water?

Sigiriya, a once-lost ancient city in Sri Lanka, was built **on top of a cliff.** Access was up stairs that led between the paws of an enormous lion statue.

Atlantis, a *legendary island* in the Atlantic Ocean said to have sunk during earthquakes, may have been inspired by the real-life fate of Pavlopetri, a *lost city in ancient* Greece.

Ancient Egyptians played the **sport** of water jousting by standing on boats and knocking opponents into the water with lances.

Soldiers during the American Revolution used cow **horns** that were specially **carved** to hold gunpowder.

Some 3,000 years ago, a Minoan **sport** likely involved running at the **horns** of a bull, then leaping over the animal.

Originally built more than 1,300 years ago in **Saudi Arabia**, Masjid al-Haram **mosque** is the world's largest mosque, holding up to four million people.

Built in 1907, the Great **Mosque** of Djenné in Mali is the largest structure made of **mud** on the planet.

Archaeologists have discovered a **mud** "cocoon" containing an Egyptian **mummy**.

Precious works of **art** were saved during World War II by a group of U.S. and British **soldiers** known as the Monuments Men (though some were women, too).

From the 16th to the mid-20th century, many artists used a pigment made from ground-up **mummies** to paint their **art**.

Archaeologists uncovered an Ice-Age mammoth tusk **carved** into the shape of two **swimming** reindeer.

To make **swimming** easier, one 1920s American invented **wooden** bathing suits.

In Victorian times, some **wooden** rocking **horses** had a secret compartment in the belly meant for hiding precious possessions.

Around the year 100, the ancient Nabataean people carved an entire city, including giant **tombs**, into huge boulders in the desert in **Saudi Arabia**.

An elaborately adorned **horse** was given a ceremonial burial in its own **tomb** nearly 3,000 years ago.

During World War I, French, British, and German **soldiers** sometimes **disguised** themselves as trees to spy on their enemies.

Disguised as a man, in 1766 French explorer Jeanne Baret became the first woman known to sail around Earth.

Adventurous discoveries

At just 16 years old, Shoshone explorer Sacagawea guided an American expedition through more than 5,000 miles (8,000km) of **wilderness**, carrying her baby the whole way.

In 1405, Chinese explorer Zheng He commanded a fleet of more than 27,000 men and more than 300 ships—including 62 ships devoted to **holding treasure**.

It's getting chilly

The Maori—Polynesian people from what is now New Zealand—may have been the first humans to **discover Antarctica**, more than 1,300 years ago.

In 1991, geologists discovered dinosaur fossils under the ice in Antarctica.

A 16th-century Ottoman map appears to show **Antarctica** without any ice, which is how the continent probably looked 6,000 years ago

Map it out

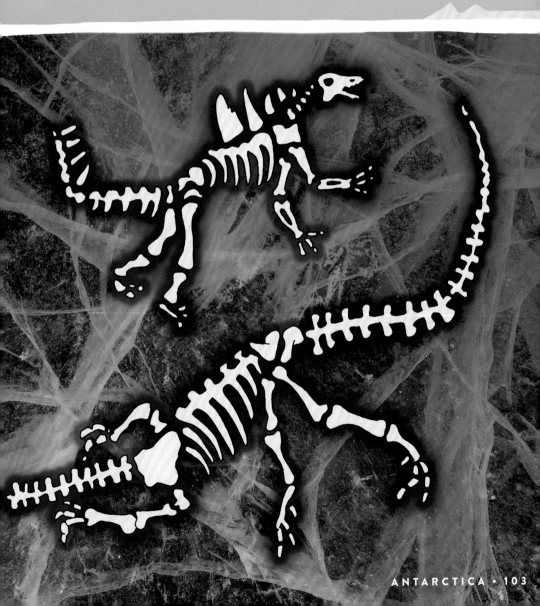

Mapmakers were able to restore a 17th-century Scottish map that had been found **inside a chimney**— where it had been for centuries.

A British map from 1793 shows England as King George III, **"pooping"** out boats to ward off a French attack...

Need the toilet?

Go to page 176

Over to ancient Mesopotamia ········>

Known as the Imago Mundi, the oldest map of the world was **carved into stone** in Mesopotamia more than 2,600 years ago

In the late 1940s, Marie Tharp became one of the first women hired by Columbia University, New York City, to be a mapmaker—but was allowed to work only as an assistant because of her gender. However, she went on to create the world's first detailed map of the **ocean floor**.

For hundreds of years, sailors living in the Pacific islands created *rebbelib*: maps made of **sticks and shells** that helped them navigate the seas

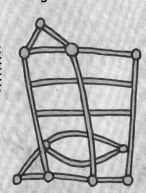

Over 3,000 years ago, people from Mesopotamia (an historical region in the Middle East) created our **concept of time**, including 60-second minutes and 60-minute hours

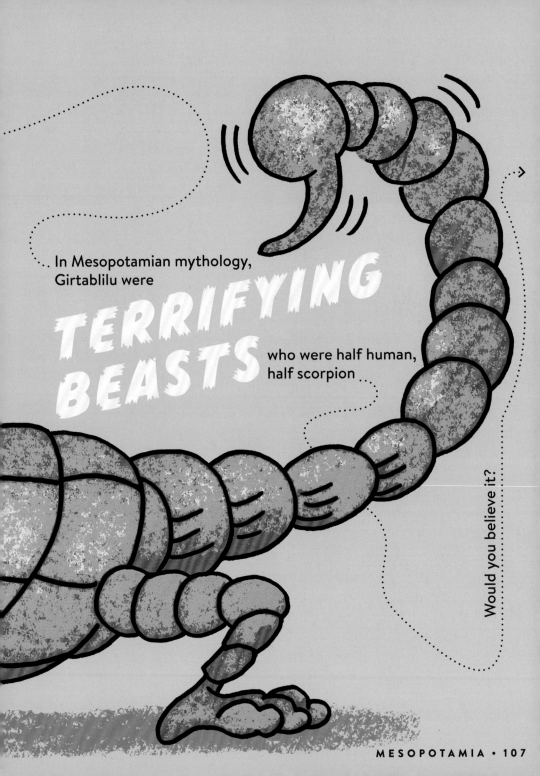

In Mesopotamian mythology, Girtablilu were

TERRIFYING BEASTS

who were half human, half scorpion

Would you believe it?

In Akan folklore—which originated in western Africa—Ananse is a **trickster spirit** who takes the form of a spider.

The god Quetzalcoatl, revered by the Aztecs of what is now central and southern Mexico, was depicted as an **enormous, feathered snake.**

In Norse mythology, Freyja, the goddess of love, rode a

CHARIOT

pulled by large cats.

Go to page 188

Terrific transportation

To honor Nekhbet, the "vulture goddess," ancient Egyptian queens sometimes wore **vulture-shaped crowns**

Dress it up

In Inuit folklore (of North America), Qallupilluit were **sea creatures** that lived under the ice and could snatch people who walked too close

Starting around the 16th century, it became popular across Southeast Asia to decorate gowns, shirts, shoes, and jewelry with

BEETLE WINGS

Brilliant bugs

Go to page 52

That's huge!

One ancient Roman author suggested using **the broth of boiled vipers** to get rid of body lice.

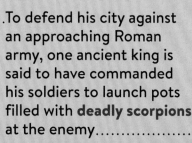

In 1812, French emperor Napoleon attempted to invade Russia, but his army fell after catching diseases from swarms of

body lice

To defend his city against an approaching Roman army, one ancient king is said to have commanded his soldiers to launch pots filled with **deadly scorpions** at the enemy.

In 1874,
the U.S.A.
experienced swarms
of **locusts** so large
they blocked out
the sun.

Turn the page

In late 16th-century Europe,
people who read a lot became
known as "**bookworms**"—after
the beetles, silverfish, and lice
that like to munch on books.

Go to page 86

More gorgeous gems

One book created in ninth-century Germany has a cover made of gold and is decorated with **precious gems**

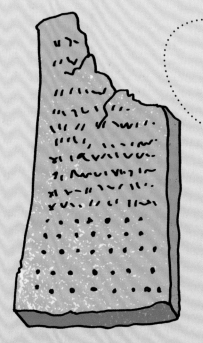

The world's **oldest known library**, in modern-day Iraq, was destroyed by a fire in 612BCE—but 30,000 books survived because they had been carved out of clay

Some of the smallest scrolls ever made were created in the eighth century when Japanese empress Shōtoku ordered one million Buddhist **prayer scrolls** to be printed for temples. Each was less than 2.5 inches (6.5cm) tall and hidden inside a pagoda-shaped charm...

Archaeologists are using lasers to read the writing on **Roman scrolls** that were buried nearly 2,000 years ago by a volcano and are too delicate to unroll...

A librarian from Timbuktu, Mali, managed to rescue 377,000 precious historical **manuscripts** when the city was invaded in 2012, transporting them more than 960 kilometres to safety...

Magnificent Mali

Go to page 150

Lead the way

Disney's *The Lion King* was likely inspired by Sundiata Keita, who founded the Mali Empire around 1240 after defeating his treacherous uncle...

Historians think that Mansa Musa, ruler of the Mali Empire in the early 1300s, was the **richest person** ever to live...

One 14th-century ruler of the Mali Empire supposedly paid the **architect** of the Djinguereber Mosque building with 441 pounds (200kg) of gold—the weight of an adult male lion

Build it →

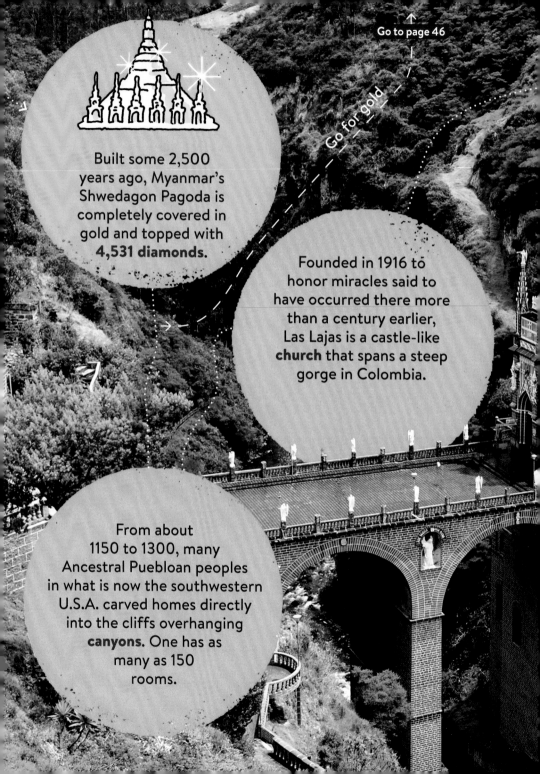

↑
Go to page 46

Go for gold

Built some 2,500 years ago, Myanmar's Shwedagon Pagoda is completely covered in gold and topped with **4,531 diamonds.**

Founded in 1916 to honor miracles said to have occurred there more than a century earlier, Las Lajas is a castle-like **church** that spans a steep gorge in Colombia.

From about 1150 to 1300, many Ancestral Puebloan peoples in what is now the southwestern U.S.A. carved homes directly into the cliffs overhanging **canyons.** One has as many as 150 rooms.

Built in the 1970s, the **Cube Houses** in the Netherlands are made from cubes built on top of concrete pillars and tilted at a 45-degree angle.

Look up

A **group of stones** more than 7,000 years old in Africa's Nubian Desert may have been the first structure on Earth built to study the skies.

For centuries, some Inuit across North America and Greenland have told stories about the cause of the **aurora borealis.** One legend says it is caused by the spirits of the dead playing a ball game—with a walrus skull as the ball.

By the late 12th century, Islamic astronomers had perfected a machine called an **astrolabe** that could calculate the time and the positions of the sun and stars.

Until the 16th century, many **doctors** in Europe thought that illnesses could be cured based on the position of the stars and planets in the sky.

Find a cure

Go to page 162

Ancient Chinese astronomers were tasked with predicting **solar eclipses**, which they believed were caused by a sky dragon eating the sun.

Journey to India

The practice of starting each new day at **midnight** may have been the idea of Aryabhata, an Indian astronomer born in 476

Historians think that the Gupta Empire
of fourth- to sixth-century India was the
first to treat **zero** as a separate number
with its own place in the numeral system

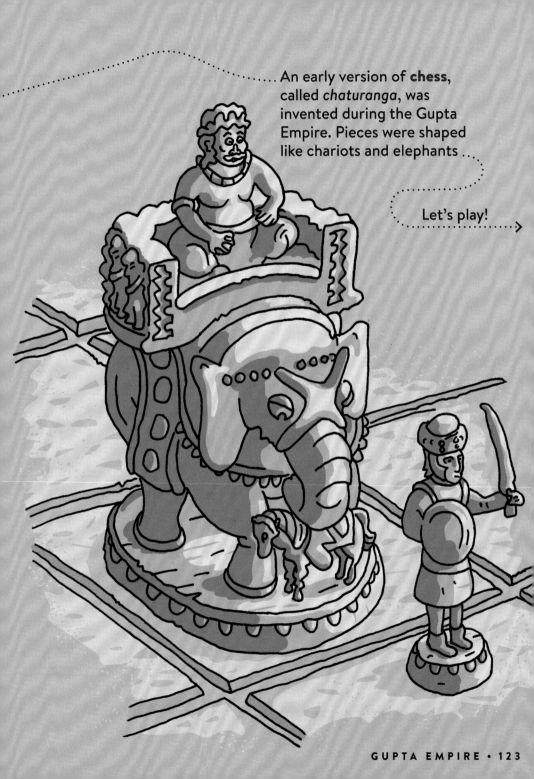

An early version of **chess**, called *chaturanga*, was invented during the Gupta Empire. Pieces were shaped like chariots and elephants...

Let's play!

Because they shed their **skin**, **snakes** were considered immortal by several ancient civilizations.

"Go" is one of the world's oldest board games; it was invented up to 4,000 years ago in **ancient China**.

People in **ancient China** may have used a mixture of animal fat and moonmilk—a mineral ooze found in caves—to moisturize their **skin**.

For more than 1,000 years, Inca in **Peru** wove strands of grass into **bridges** to enable them to cross steep mountain gorges.

The ancient Egyptians believed that they would be protected from **snakes** and scorpions by the cat goddess Mafdet.

In ancient Greek mythology, the goddess Athena turned a woman into a spider because the woman **wove** a better tapestry than she did.

Archaeologists found more than 40 mummified dogs in a 1,000-year-old pet cemetery in Lima, **Peru**.

Until sometime around the 1800s, the Salish people of North America **wove** blankets and clothes from the fur of a now extinct breed of dog.

A French **castle** built some 900 years ago is twice the size it looks—nearly half of it is underground!

In 2021, archaeologists found the remains of a 13th-century bridge thought to have been part of Eye **Castle** in Suffolk, U.K.

Go deeper

According to legend, catacombs b[u]
housing the dead deep under Alexa[ndria]
Egypt, were rediscovered in 1900 v[when]
a **donkey** fell through a hole above

In the 13th century, Polish salt-mine workers **carved their workplace** in Wieliczka to look like a building. It eventually had nine levels, chandeliers, and a church—all carved from the salt

Noushabad is an ancient underground city in Iran that was carved by hand. It had many **hidden entrances**, including some tucked behind ovens in people's homes

More buildings

Go to page 118

British archaeologists discovered the

LOST
REMAINS

of 15th-century King Richard III
buried under a parking lot

What a find!

Scientists diving in the Aegean Sea located an ancient Greek shipwreck full of 2,400-year-old jars. After using a robot to carefully collect the jars, they discovered what was inside: very old salad dressing.

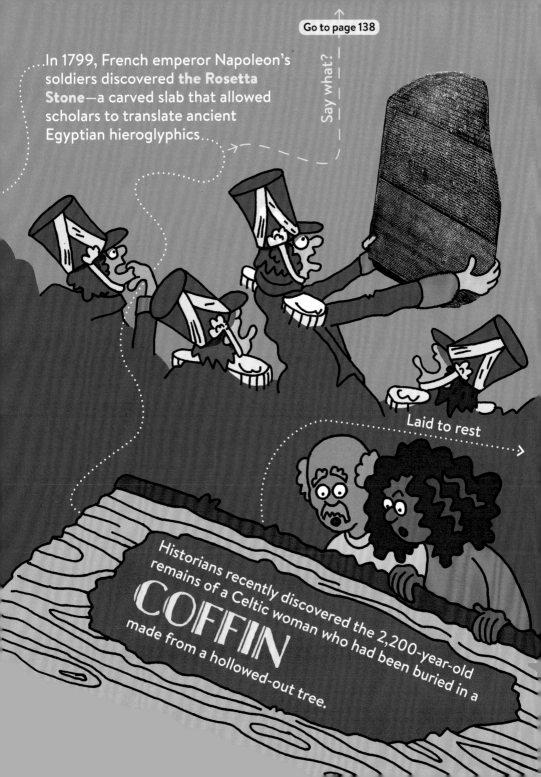

Go to page 138

Say what?

In 1799, French emperor Napoleon's soldiers discovered **the Rosetta Stone**—a carved slab that allowed scholars to translate ancient Egyptian hieroglyphics...

Laid to rest

Historians recently discovered the 2,200-year-old remains of a Celtic woman who had been buried in a **COFFIN** made from a hollowed-out tree.

.....India's famous Taj Mahal is a **mausoleum** housing
the burial place of Emperor Shāh Jahān's beloved wife.
It took more than 1,000 elephants to transport all
the materials to build the structure.....

.....Thought to be
the resting place
of the legendary
Japanese emperor
Nintoku, Daisen Kofun
is an enormous
fifth-century
burial mound shaped like
a keyhole and
surrounded by moats.....

Go to page 84

Seeing skeletons

OSSEMENS DE L'EGLISE
ET DU CLOITRE DES
CAPUCINS S HONORE
LE 20 MARS 1804

The **catacombs** of Paris—ancient underground tunnels converted in 1786 to hold skeletons—are thought to stretch for over 186 miles (300km).

Beware!

During the Han dynasty of ancient China, many rulers and nobles were buried in suits made of a **green stone** called jade.

The deaths of several people associated with digging up King Tutankhamun's tomb led people to believe it was cursed.

After buying the

HOPE DIAMOND

necklace in 1911, American socialite Evalyn
Walsh McLean learned that it was supposedly
cursed. Even so, Evalyn would put the
necklace on her Great Dane or play
scavenger hunts where she "lost" the gem
and encouraged guests to her home to find it

So beautiful!

Go to page 58

...While performing Fon Lep, an ancient dance from northern Thailand, dancers wear brass **finger jewelry** designed to look like long, pointed nails....

...Women in late 19th-century Europe and the Americas sometimes decorated their hair with **fireflies**...........

Hair raising!

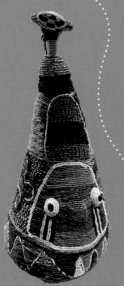

...West African Yoruba rulers have for centuries worn elaborate **beaded crowns** that are said to protect their subjects from the supernatural power that radiates from a ruler's face...........

Some Victorian **hair combs** were made from celluloid—a type of plastic that will explode if it gets too hot

High-ranking Inca wore heavy **gold earrings** that would stretch their earlobes as a symbol of nobility

Some 800 years ago, the Inca developed a way to **preserve potatoes** by freeze-drying them—just as we preserve some foods today.

Inca architects designed many of their buildings, including Machu Picchu, high up in the mountains of Peru, to be mostly

EArThQuAkE-pRoOf

Inca messengers, called chasquis, used a **relay system** that allowed them to send messages from person to person up to 250 miles (402km) per day..........

Tell me about it!

The Inca ruler Sapa Inca would wear an item of clothing, then the next day he would **BURN IT**.

The Inca used a system of **knotted ropes**, called *quipus*, to record information...

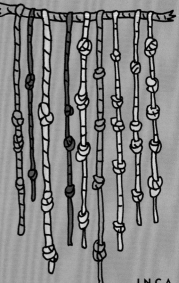

One of the oldest known references to sign language was written by an ancient Greek philosopher more than 2,400 years ago

For some 1,000 years,

Beat it! →

people in western Africa have used "talking drums" that can copy human speech and send messages up to 20 miles (32km) away

In Ansai, China, waist drum dancing (leaping and dancing while playing drums) was created more than 2,000 years ago and is still used to celebrate the Lunar New Year.

In a Romanian tradition from at least the 1700s, a group of young men would ring in the New Year with one of them disguised as a **goat** and dancing at each doorstep in their village.

A giant **ship** built more than 2,000 years ago in Sicily, Italy, was so **long** that it couldn't dock anywhere on the island and had to be given away.

A centuries-old superstition says that if you don't break up the shell after eating an **egg**, a witch can use the shell as a boat and cause danger to **ships**.

Measuring more than 240 feet (73m) **long**, Egypt's Sphinx sculpture was carved from one enormous block of **stone** more than 4,500 years ago.

For millennia across Europe and Asia, a semiprecious **stone** called lapis lazuli was ground up to make a rare blue **paint**.

A yellow **paint** color created in India in the 15th century was supposedly made using urine from **cows** that had been fed only mango leaves.

Art from nearly 3,000 years ago shows an Assyrian soldier using an inflated **goat** stomach to help him float while **swimming**.

Swimming or taking a boat is the only way to get to the oldest **cemetery** in Camiguin, in the Philippines, because the cemetery sank following a volcanic eruption in the 1870s.

At one ancient Siberian **cemetery**, scientists discovered people buried alongside dog and **wolf** companions.

In 1807, a Genoese sailor **founded** Tavolara, an island off Italy's Sardinian coast, which remains the smallest **kingdom** in the world.

According to legend, a **wolf** raised two human babies who, when they grew up, **founded** the city of Rome.

Legend says that a Chinese princess first brought silk to the Central Asian **kingdom** of Khotan by smuggling silkworm **eggs** from China hidden in her headdress.

Set sail

A breed of **cow** that could grow larger than a horse went extinct in 1627, but **scientists** are studying its DNA and may bring it back.

Scientists think that nearly 300 years before Christopher Columbus reached the Americas, Polynesian people and Indigenous Americans met while exploring the oceans.

For hundreds of years, Chinese naval forces included a *louchuan*, a sort of **floating, fortified castle** complete with huge catapults...

Go to page 80

To the castle!

According to legend, the *Flying Dutchman* is a **ghost ship** that roams the waters off South Africa's Cape of Good Hope, where it sank

Boo!

The oldest known ghost story was written more than 3,000 years ago in ancient Egypt

For centuries, visitors to the Tower of London have claimed to see the ghost of Anne Boleyn, the English queen who was beheaded by her husband King Henry VIII

From the 1880s to the 1920s in Victoria, Australia, groups of "ghost hoaxers" used sheets to dress up as spooky spirits and scare passersby

Head down under ⟩

The **didgeridoo**—an instrument made from tree branches or roots that have been hollowed by termites—has been played by Aboriginal people for thousands of years.

When they first learned about it, 18th-century British scientists thought that the **platypus**—a strange-looking animal native to Australia—was a prank.

In the 1950s, an Australian architect was
inspired to build Sydney's world-renowned

OPERA HOUSE

after peeling an orange....

Dig in!

In August 1661, King Louis XIV of France was the guest of honor at a **lavish feast**—with food, performances, and fireworks—and put his host in prison soon after.

The first meal that astronauts ate on the moon included **bacon**.

Modern-day **ketchup** is a version of an ancient Chinese sauce, called *kê-tsiap*, made from fermented fish.

Go to page 16

Enter the pyramid

U.S. President George H.W. Bush once banned **broccoli** from all his meals

... Archaeologists found **watermelon seeds** in King Tut's tomb that were nearly 4,000 years old ...

Lead the way!

During World War II, Britain's Queen Elizabeth II, then a princess, trained as a **TRUCK MECHANIC**

In 1990, Violeta Barrios de Chamorro went right from running a newspaper to becoming president of Nicaragua and the **first female president** in all of Central America

The **Indian queen** Lakshmi Bai led an uprising against the British army when she was just 22

Trot on!

Go to page 12

Nineteenth-century French emperor Napoleon Bonaparte was once attacked— and defeated— by a mob of

HUNGRY BUNNIES

Nelson Mandela, a revolutionary who became South Africa's first Black president in 1994, once dressed as a **chauffeur** to escape the authorities

Time for a revolution

The Trung sisters led a rebellion against the Chinese rule of Vietnam in the first century, and are often shown riding elephants into battle

Toussaint Louverture, an 18th-century formerly enslaved man, led a rebellion that would successfully **abolish slavery** in Haiti. He became the country's first Black leader.

In 18th-century Jamaica, groups of formerly enslaved people led by a woman called Queen Nanny founded **hidden towns** in the jungles and mountains...

During the Qing dynasty in China, Qiu Jin dressed in traditionally male clothing, left the country to attend school, learned sword fighting, and led a revolt for **women's equality**...

Queen Boudicca, leader of the Celtic **Iceni tribe** during the first century in Britain, led an army against the powerful Roman Empire. Her army seized three towns and almost drove the Romans out of Britain...

Meet the Celts

Halloween comes from the ancient Celtic holiday Samhain, a time when spirits were believed to be close by

Go to page 144

Spooky

Meow

In Celtic mythology, the cat-sith was a cat fairy that could grant blessings or steal souls.

Go to page 178

Squeak, squeak!

In 1949, a **ship's cat** named

SIMON

was awarded a medal for raising morale and keeping ships rat free

The **khao manee cat** was bred more than 600 years ago as a pet for royal families in Thailand

According to one historian, ancient Egyptians kept **lions in temples** and sang while feeding them. Some of the lions were mummified when they died...

Keeping mum

The 2,100-year-old mummy of a Chinese noblewoman was so well preserved that she still had **BLOOD** in her veins

...A man who lived more than 5,000 years ago was naturally mummified by the **freezing temperatures** of the Alps mountains in Europe—and you can still see his tattoos......

Some 7,000 years ago, people in what is now Chile created mummies by **painting them** with a mineral called manganese.

In the cold

Go to page 76

Miners in Iran discovered the remains of people who were mummified in a **salt mine** more than 1,700 years ago...

Off to ancient Egypt

...The ancient Egyptians sometimes mummified **snakes**...

The ancient Egyptians invented a version of bowling.

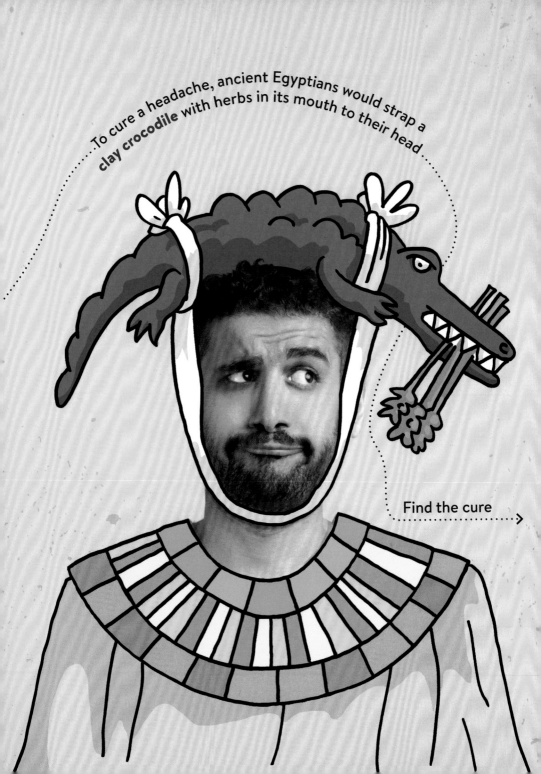

To cure a headache, ancient Egyptians would strap a clay **crocodile** with herbs in its mouth to their head

Find the cure ·····›

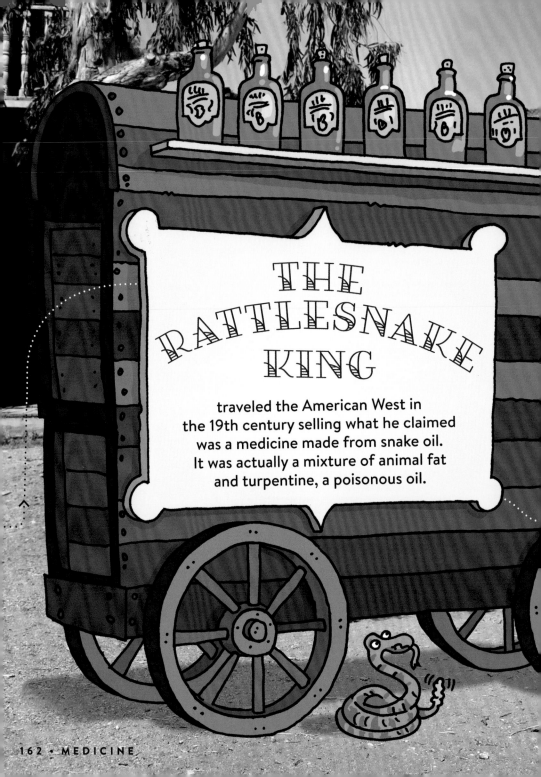

THE RATTLESNAKE KING

traveled the American West in
the 19th century selling what he claimed
was a medicine made from snake oil.
It was actually a mixture of animal fat
and turpentine, a poisonous oil.

To the Wild West

In 1862, during the **gold rush** in British Columbia, Canada, Bactrian **camels** were imported to help haul supplies and loot.

Camels were popular transportation on the Silk **Road**, which connected China and the Roman Empire. It was 4,000 miles (6,437km) long!

Much of San Francisco is built on top of **ships** that were abandoned after the 19th-century **gold rush** in California.

In the late 1800s in **New Zealand**, a dolphin that came to be named Pelorus Jack accompanied **ships** as they sailed in and out of the bay.

Mary Fields was the first female mail carrier in the Wild West and was said to be so tough she once fought off a pack of **wolves**.

Many of the **roads** built in the American Southwest by Ancestral Puebloans are so straight that instead of going around cliffs or mountains, they travel vertically up the face of the rock.

Meet the Ancestral Puebloans

A mechanical **clock** in New Zealand has been running since 1864 without ever being wound up.

Shaped like an elephant with human and animal riders, a **clock** created by inventor Al-Jazari in the Islamic Empire included a mechanical bird that chirped every half hour.

Before the arrival of the Celts, a people known as the Wuffinga, or "kin of wolves," were the **rulers** of a kingdom in eastern England.

Gifts given by other **rulers** to England's King Henry III included leopards, a polar bear, and an elephant.

To survive droughts, Ancestral Puebloans likely obtained water by **melting ice** they collected from empty lava tubes....

....Ancestral Puebloans wove blankets from **turkey feathers,** using the same heat-trapping technology found in modern down jackets and quilts..........

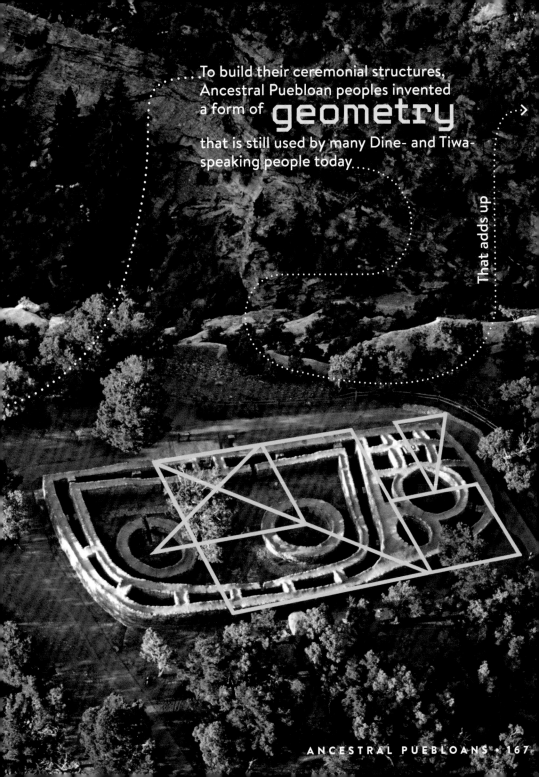

To build their ceremonial structures, Ancestral Puebloan peoples invented a form of **geometry** that is still used by many Dine- and Tiwa-speaking people today.

That adds up

In the 1950s, to test pilot safety at supersonic speeds, U.S. scientist John Paul Stapp strapped himself to a  **ROCKET-POWERED SLED.** He reached more than 600 miles an hour (966km/h)—and survived.

The **ham sandwich theorem**, a mathematical rule from the 1940s, states that it is always possible to slice a ham sandwich equally in two with just one cut.

Eat up

Pythagoreanism, a study of mathematical ideas, began as a cult devoted to **mystical numbers**.

Go to page 148

In the Islamic Empire in the ninth century, mathematician Muhammad Al-Khwarizmi, known as the **Father of Algebra**, created the math that would later be used for flight, space travel, and coding....

An age of wonders

In the 1960s, a group of African-American women were responsible for calculating by hand the math that **NASA** needed to send astronauts to space....

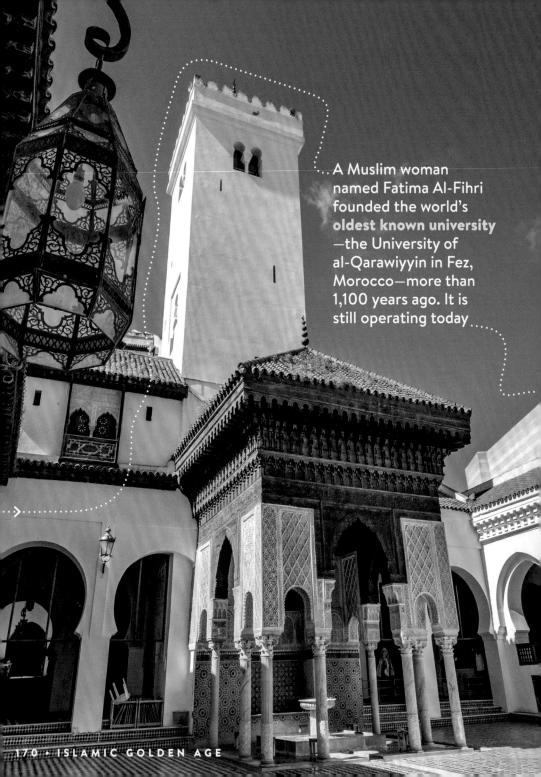

A Muslim woman named Fatima Al-Fihri founded the world's **oldest known university** —the University of al-Qarawiyyin in Fez, Morocco—more than 1,100 years ago. It is still operating today

According to legend, the ninth-century musician Ziryab was so talented that he was forced to leave his homeland in what is now Iraq and travel to Spain because his music teacher had become too

JEALOUS

Making music >

In the mythology of Bali, the king of all good **spirits** is Barong, a lion-like creature who **dances** to fend off evil.

In Hawaii, the hula **dance** has been used throughout history to tell stories about stars, the weather, and **volcanic activity**.

The *mbira* is a piano-like musical instrument traditionally used by the Shona people of Zimbabwe to contact **spirits**.

In 1917, a **toilet** went down in history as a work of art after an **artist** turned it upside down and signed it.

Explosions sometimes happened if too much gas built up in ancient Roman **toilets**.

Italian Renaissance **artist** Leonardo da Vinci created a design for a giant **crossbow**.

According to legend, there are **crossbow** booby traps inside the **tomb** of the first emperor of China's Qin dynasty.

For at least 100 years, Icelandic people have used the heat from **volcanic activity** to bake **bread**.

Stale pieces of **bread** called "trenchers" were used as plates in the **Middle Ages.**

In the **Middle Ages** it was thought that a substance called the philosopher's stone could produce **immortality** potions.

Early Chinese scientists searching for a potion to give you **immortality** caused **explosions**—and accidentally invented gunpowder.

That's ancient!

Archaeologists in China found a 3,300-year-old pair of **pants**—the oldest ever discovered.

From 1800 until 2013, it was officially **illegal** for women to wear **pants** in Paris, France.

The terracotta army also in the **tomb** of Emperor Qin Shihuangdi included 600 life-size terracotta **horses.**

According to one English writer, to protect the town of Newmarket's **horses** from getting sick, it became **illegal** for people to blow their noses in public.

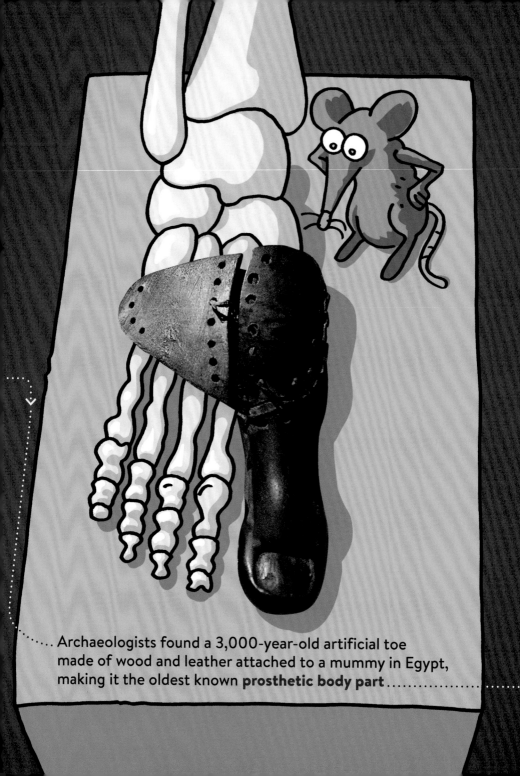

Archaeologists found a 3,000-year-old artificial toe made of wood and leather attached to a mummy in Egypt, making it the oldest known **prosthetic body part**

The world's oldest known

PILLOW,

created in Mesopotamia
around 9,000 years ago,
was made from stone...

...Scientists discovered one of the world's oldest
running-water toilets in a 2,000-year-old tomb!
It was likely added as a restroom for the afterlife

The bathroom in a European medieval castle had a space for hanging clothes. They believed the

ammonia

from pee would kill fleas.

The first toilet in a **space shuttle** was a hole on the side of the shuttle wall with collection bags on the other side.

In 1902, there were so many **rats** in the sewers of Hanoi, Vietnam, that they started climbing out of people's toilets..........

Smell a rat?

In a 15th-century temple in Rajasthan, India, some

20,000 RATS

are worshipped and fed milk

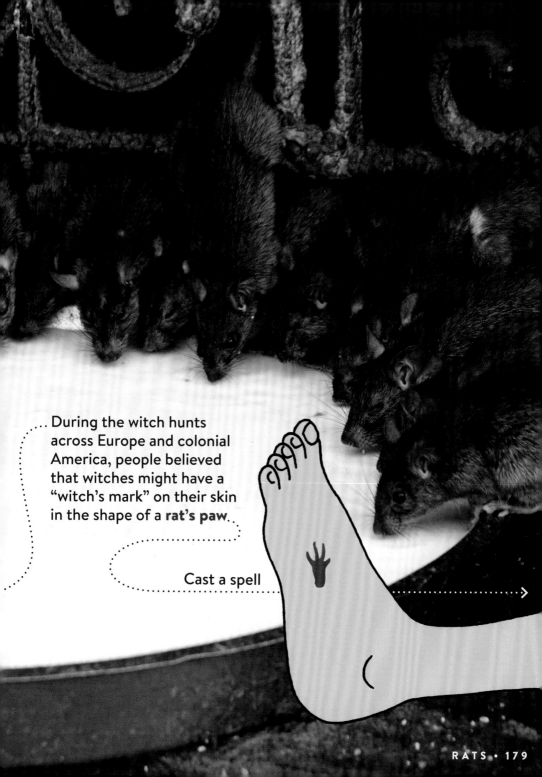

During the witch hunts across Europe and colonial America, people believed that witches might have a "witch's mark" on their skin in the shape of a **rat's paw**.

Cast a spell

In Russian folklore, Baba Yaga is an

EViL WiTCH

who steals children. She lives in a hut with giant chicken legs, and she flies around in an iron pot.

Time for a brew >

According to legend, Emperor Shen Nung of China discovered tea when the wind accidentally **blew leaves** from a tree into his pot of boiling water.

Several Indigenous nations across North America drank a caffeinated tea made from **holly tree leaves**.

While cleaning out his garage, a British man discovered an **18th-century container** shaped like a tea pot that sold for nearly £400,000 (about $520,000)

Lost loot

Go to page 186

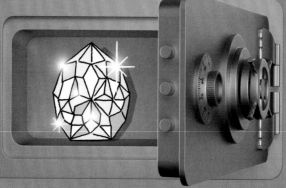

In 1918, the royal family of Austria deposited an enormous **yellow diamond** into a Swiss bank vault—but it went missing, never to be seen again...

It's said that pirates who attacked a 19th-century Spanish ship fled with **1.5 million gold coins**—which they lost when they were caught in a storm and marooned on a deserted island...

In 1907, the Irish crown jewels were stolen from Dublin Castle—and have never been found...

Go to page 22

In 1608, a Portuguese explorer tried to steal Myanmar's Dhammazedi Bell, the **largest bell** in the world. Made from copper, silver, and gold, it was too heavy for his raft and it sank into the sea

In 1981, a construction worker in Mexico City discovered what may be some Aztec **gold** that was stolen by Spanish invaders nearly 500 years ago

Stop, thief!

In 1899, a group of Wild West outlaws known as the Wild Bunch **blew up a bridge** and stole nearly $1 million in today's money from the train that was forced to stop ...

Follow the track ⟶

According to one account, in 1830 a U.S. businessman tried to prove the power of locomotives by racing his train against a horse—but the

HORSE WON

Go to page 12

Ride this way

Above the busiest train station in Australia is an abandoned 1899 ballroom so secret that only people who have received rare "golden tickets" have been able to view it.

Shall we dance?

Since the early 20th century, Anishinaabe people in Canada and the U.S. Upper Midwest have performed the **Jingle Dress Dance**—which features dresses made with jingling metal cones—to channel healing for those who are sick.

During the whirling dervish, a Sufi form of meditation created in the 13th century, dancers can spin for several hours without **getting dizzy**.

In the 1920s, a U.S. dancer named Frankie Manning invented a dance move called **the aerial** when he flipped his dance partner over his back.

At the centuries-old Gerewol Festival, in Chad, Wodaabe men dance for hours under the harsh desert sun to show off their **endurance**

On top of being skilled in battle, medieval European **knights** were also expected to know how to dance

How gallant!

To the desert

Go to page 74

In full armor, most British knights were

TOO
HEAVY

for the local horses. So until the 1500s, larger breeds were brought in from other countries to carry them.............

...... A knight's full suit of armor could weigh up to 110 pounds (50kg)— that's like carrying about **nine bowling balls** on your back......

Strike! ➤

In 1935, a Romanian artist began adding **paintings** and poems to the tombstones of a graveyard known as the Merry Cemetery.

The notes of a music piece may be hidden in one of Leonardo da Vinci's **paintings**.

Centuries-old Tuvan **throat** singing is a form of music in which people can sing more than one note simultaneously.

An early version of bowling began as a religious ceremony in Europe some 1,700 years ago.

In medieval Europe, the nobility often wore shoes that were so long the **toes** had to be supported with stuffing.

In 1870, when its graveyard became too full, a church in what is now Czechia was converted into a tomb, featuring art made from human **bones**.

More than 7,000 years ago, **bones** were used as dice in ancient Mesopotamia.

The dice game Perudo comes from the ancient Peruvian game Dudo.

A British folk remedy prescribed wrapping sweaty socks around your neck to cure a sore **throat**.

Let's play!

Ancient Egyptians may have kept their **toes** cozy in socks with two separate toe sections.

SCORE
25

Tetris was the first video game played in space.

One of the oldest known board games is the **Royal Game of Ur.** Played more than 4,000 years ago in Mesopotamia, the winner was the person who could race their piece to the end of the board first ...

You've reached...

According to some historians, Roman soldiers played a form of **hopscotch** in their armor to improve their speed and reflexes...

In 18th-century France, theaters hired **groups of claqueurs:** people paid to cry and laugh at the right moments and applaud at the end of a show to encourage the rest of the audience to join in.

Glossary of historical terms

Ancestor: A dead relation, such as your great grandmother's grandmother. "Ancestors" are also earlier generations of a whole group or tribe.

Archaeologist: A person who researches human societies of earlier times by studying things left behind such as coins, graves, and ruined buildings.

BCE: An abbreviation for "Before Common Era"—the period dating before year 1, based on the Christian calendar.

CE: An abbreviation for "Common Era"—the period dating from year 1, based on the Christian calendar.

Century: A period of one hundred years.

Ceremony: A formal event or ritual, for example, as part of a religion or to celebrate something.

Civilization: A group of people who share certain advanced ways of living and working.

Colony: A city founded, or a region settled, by people from another country. Colonies are usually partly controlled by the country from which the settlers came.

Empire: A type of political unit. Throughout history, countries have wanted to take control of lands and peoples beyond their borders. This practice is called imperialism, and the lands that they take control of are called an empire. The ruler of an empire is sometimes called an emperor.

Ethnic: A social group or category of the population that is set apart from other groups in a society. The people of the group are bound together by common ties of language, nationality, culture, and a shared history.

Folklore: Ancient customs, tales, sayings, dances, or art forms preserved among a people, and carried from one generation to the next by word of mouth.

Indigenous people: The original inhabitants of an area and their descendants.

Legend: A story from long ago that may or may not be based on truth.

Manuscript: A handwritten book.

Mummy: A dead body that has been partly preserved by special treatments to prevent decay.

Mythology: A set of stories, often about gods or legendary figures, belonging to a particular ancient civilization or tribe.

Province: A large region of a country, often with its own culture and traditions.

Settlers: People who make their home in new areas.

Glossary of cultures, civilizations, peoples & periods

Aboriginal people: One out of two groups of Indigenous people in Australia (the other group being the Torres Strait Islander peoples). Aboriginal peoples descended from humans who reached the continent around 40,000–80,000 years ago.

Akan people: A group of peoples who speak any of the Akan languages, originating along the coast of western Africa.

Ancestral Puebloan people: A civilization that existed in the southwestern U.S.A. from about 100 to about 1600. Descendants of the Ancestral Puebloans inhabit Arizona, Colorado, New Mexico, and Utah today.

Anishinaabe people: A large cultural group of Indigenous and First Nations peoples living in the Great Lakes region of the U.S.A. and Canada. This group includes nations who were also given other names by colonizers, such as the Ojibwe or Chippewa.

Assyrian civilization: A Mesopotamian civilization that existed from 14th–7th century BCE in what is now Iraq and southeastern Turkey.

Aztec civilization: In or around 1325, a group of people known as the Aztecs established an empire in what is now central Mexico. In the 1500s, Spanish explorers and troops invaded Central and South America, bringing disease and devastation. The Aztec Empire was conquered in 1521.

Celts: The Celts were a collection of tribes and peoples who spoke Indo-European languages and lived in Europe beginning at least 2,500 years ago. The Celts eventually migrated throughout much of Europe, and their heritage remains in many places throughout Britain.

Cherokee Nation: An Indigenous nation that originally inhabited much of the southeast U.S.A.. Though they are now commonly known as Cherokee, people of the nation traditionally refer to themselves as Aniyvwiya.

Chickasaw Nation: An Indigenous nation originally based in what is now Mississippi, Alabama, Tennessee, and Kentucky in the U.S.A. The Chickasaw people were forcibly relocated to Oklahoma in 1832 after being forced to sell their lands to the U.S. government.

Diné language: An Athabaskan language spoken by Indigenous nations in the southwestern U.S.A. These nations include the Navajo and Apache, who both refer to themselves as Diné.

Etruscan civilization: A civilization that existed in what is now Italy from about 800 BCE to about 300 BCE.

Gupta Empire: A civilization that ruled what is now northern India from the 4th century to the 6th.

Han dynasty: A family of rulers who oversaw China from 206 BCE to 220 CE.

Hopi tribe: An Indigenous nation, also known as the Hopituh Shi-nu-mu, who originally inhabited what is now Arizona. They are the descendants of the Ancestral Puebloans.

Iceni tribe: A Celtic tribe that lived in parts of what is now Britain. The Iceni were largely conquered by the ancient Romans in the 1st century.

Inca civilization: An Andean civilization that inhabited an empire in what is now Peru from the 13th–16th centuries. In the early 1500s,

Spanish explorers and troops invaded Central and South America, bringing disease and devastation. The Inca empire was conquered in 1572.

Inuit people: A group of Indigenous peoples who originally inhabited the Arctic regions of what are now Canada, Russia, Greenland, and the U.S.A.

Islamic Golden Age: A period of history from the 8th century to the 16th century during which scientists, artists, and other visionaries within the Islamic world made great contributions to science, math, art, and more.

Itsekiri people: An ethnic group of people originally from what is now Nigeria.

Kingdom of Khotan: A Buddhist kingdom located in what is now China from about the 3rd century BCE to the 10th century CE.

Mali Empire: An empire that existed in western Africa from around 1000–1600 CE.

Mangbetu people: An ethnic group of peoples who originally inhabited central Africa.

Māori people: One of several groups of Polynesian peoples who originally inhabited the islands of Polynesia. Maori people have traditionally lived in what is now New Zealand since the 14th century.

Maya civilization: An Indigenous society in Mexico and Central America, thought to have existed since around 1500 BCE. Today the Maya population is around six million.

Mesopotamia: A historical region in what is now Iraq and Kuwait, as well as parts of Iran, Syria, and Turkey.

Middle Ages: The period in European history that came between ancient and modern times. It lasted from about 500 CE to about 1500 CE.

Minoan civilization: A civilization that existed on what is now Crete, an island in Greece, from about 3000 BCE to about 1100 BCE.

Moche people: An ancient civilization that existed from 1st–8th century in what is now northern Peru.

Mongol Empire: One of the world's largest empires, existing from 1206–1368 across much of Asia.

Nabataean Kingdom: A kingdom that existed in the region of modern-day Jordan from the 4th century BCE to the 2nd century CE.

Norse people: A group of Germanic language-speaking peoples, also known as Vikings, who originally inhabited Scandinavia and colonized and raided other parts of Europe from about the 9th–11th century.

Nubian Desert: An eastern region of the Sahara in Sudan.

Ottoman Empire: An Islamic and Turkish empire that ruled in parts of Europe, Asia, and Africa and expanded from the 14th–17th century.

Persian Empire: Also called the Achaemenid Empire, an empire that ruled parts of Asia and Africa from around 550–330 BCE.

Polynesian people: An ethnic group of peoples who first inhabited Polynesia some 3,000 years ago.

Qin dynasty: The family of rulers in China from 221–207 BCE.

Qing dynasty: The family of rulers in China from 1644–1911/1912.

Salish people: A group of Indigenous nations and tribes originally inhabiting what is now southwestern Canada and the northwestern U.S.A.

Sami people: Indigenous people who speak the Sami language and originally inhabited areas of northern Europe and what is now Russia.

Scythian civilization: A nomadic empire that existed in Central Asia and what are now Russia and Ukraine from about 900 to about 200 BCE.

Seminole tribe: An Indigenous tribe originally inhabiting what are now Florida and Georgia in the U.S.A.

Shona people: An ethnic group of peoples who speak Bantu languages, originally from southern Africa.

Shoshone people: An Indigenous band of peoples who originally inhabited what is now the western U.S.A.

Soviet Union: A country that existed from 1922–1991 over large parts of Asia and eastern Europe.

Sufism: A body of Islamic religious practice.

Tiwa language: A language spoken by Indigenous Puebloan peoples of the southwestern U.S.A.

Tlingit people: Indigenous peoples who originally inhabited what is now Alaska and parts of western Canada.

Tuareg people: Nomadic Berber-speaking peoples originally from areas in northern and western Africa.

Tuvan people: Also called Tyvan, an ethnic group of peoples originally from parts of Russia and Mongolia.

Vikings: See "Norse people."

Visigoths: A group of Germanic peoples originally from what is now Romania who conquered the Roman Empire in the 4th century.

Wodaabe people: A nomadic tribe of people from Central Africa.

Wuffingas dynasty: The ruling family of parts of what is now eastern England in the 6th–8th century.

Yoruba people: An ethnic group of peoples originally from what is now Nigeria, Benin, and northern Togo.

Yupik people: Indigenous Arctic people traditionally residing in Siberia, St. Lawrence Island, and the Diomede Islands in the Bering Sea and Bering Strait, and Alaska.

Meet the FACTopians

Paige Towler is an author and editor based in Washington, D.C. A former editor for National Geographic Kids Books, she writes poetry about animals doing yoga, weird facts about the world, and silly stories about snakes and bats. When thinking about which historical facts to include in *History FACTopia*, Paige took inspiration from all her favorite subjects: mysteries, forgotten and little-known history, food, fashion, and more. Her favorite fact in this book is that one king in ancient Iran supposedly launched clay pots full of scorpions at his enemies.

Andy Smith is an award-winning illustrator. A graduate of the Royal College of Art, London, U.K., he creates artwork that has an optimistic, handmade feel. Creating the illustrations for *History FACTopia* brought even more surprises, from aliens in Roswell to warring emus! His favorite fact to draw was Nian, the monster with a lion's head. Inspired by the man who found a valuable container in his garage, Andy searched in his shed but found only lawnmower parts and an old doorknob.

Lawrence Morton is an art director and designer based in London, U.K. He carefully created the trail that guides you through this book. He has a little dachshund named Charley and loved learning about Nepal's Kukur Tihar festival.

Sources

Scientists, historians, and other experts are discovering new facts and updating information all the time. That's why our *FACTopia* team has checked that every fact that appears in this book is based on multiple trustworthy sources and has been verified by a team of Britannica fact-checkers. Of the hundreds of sources used in this book, here is a list of key websites we consulted.

News Organizations

archaeology.org
bbc.com
bbc.co.uk
businessinsider.com
cnn.com
Earthsky.org
forbes.com
Heritagedaily.com
Latimes.com
livescience.com
nationalgeographic.com
nationalgeographic.org
nbcnews.com
newscientist.com
npr.org
nytimes.com
pbs.org
phys.org
sciencealert.com
sciencedaily.com
scientificamerican.com
theatlantic.com
theguardian.com
washingtonpost.com
wsj.com
zmescience.com

Government, Scientific, and Academic Organizations

britannica.com
cdc.gov
gutenberg.org
encyclopedia.com
journals.plos.org
jstor.org
link.springer.com
loc.gov
nasa.gov
nps.gov
nature.com
ncbi.nlm.nih.gov
oxfordreference.com
publicdomainreview.org
pubmed.ncbi.nlm.nih.gov
researchgate.net
whc.unesco.org

Museums and Zoos

americanindian.si.edu
americanhistory.si.edu
africa.si.edu
britishmuseum.org
brooklynmuseum.org
historymuseum.ca
learninglab.si.edu
marinersmuseum.org
metmuseum.org
nms.ac.uk
si.edu
smithsonianmag.com

Universities

cambridge.org
byu.edu
mcgill.ca
psu.edu
uchicago.edu
washington.edu

Other Websites

akc.org
ancient-origins.net
atlasobscura.com
cbc.ca
english-heritage.org
guinnessworldrecords.com
history.com
historic-uk.com
khanacademy.org
kids.kiddle.co
lonelyplanet.com
mexicolore.co.uk
thespruceeats.com
thevintagenews.com
tripadvisor.com
worldhistory.org

Picture Credits

The publisher would like to thank the following for permission to reproduce their photographs and illustrations. While every effort has been made to credit images, the publisher apologizes for any errors or omissions and will be pleased to make any necessary corrections in future editions of the book.

Index

BRITANNICA
BOOKS

Britannica Books is an imprint of What on Earth Publishing,
published in collaboration with Britannica, Inc.
Allington Castle, Maidstone, Kent ME16 0NB, United Kingdom
30 Ridge Road Unit B, Greenbelt, Maryland, 20770, United States

First published in the United States in 2023

Written by Paige Towler
Illustrated by Andy Smith
Designed by Lawrence Morton
Edited by Kate Hale
Sensitivity read by Jordan Merica, Salt & Sage Books
Indexed by Vanessa Bird

Encyclopaedia Britannica
Alison Eldridge, Managing Editor; Michele Rita Metych, Fact-checking Supervisor;
Will Gosner, Fact-checker

Britannica Books
Nancy Feresten, Publisher; Natalie Bellos, Editorial Director; Meg Osborne, Editor;
Andy Forshaw, Art Director; Lauren Fulbright, Production Director

Library of Congress Cataloging-in-Publication Data available upon request

ISBN: 9781804660416

Printed in India
RP/Haryana, India/02/2023

13 5 7 9 10 8 6 4 2

whatonearthbooks.com
britannica-books.com

MIX
Paper from
responsible sources
FSC® C016779